THE SQUIRREL

To Octavius   M.L.

To Kathy   K.L.

Library of Congress Catalog Card Number 81-1229
Printed in Italy
First Pied Piper Printing 1982
A Pied Piper Book is a registered trademark of The Dial Press.
First published in Great Britain in 1981 by Methuen/Walker Books

THE SQUIRREL is published in a hardcover edition by The Dial Press,
1 Dag Hammarskjold Plaza, New York, New York 10017.
ISBN 0-8037-8330-2

THE
SQUIRREL

By Margaret Lane

Pictures by
Kenneth Lilly

THE DIAL PRESS/New York

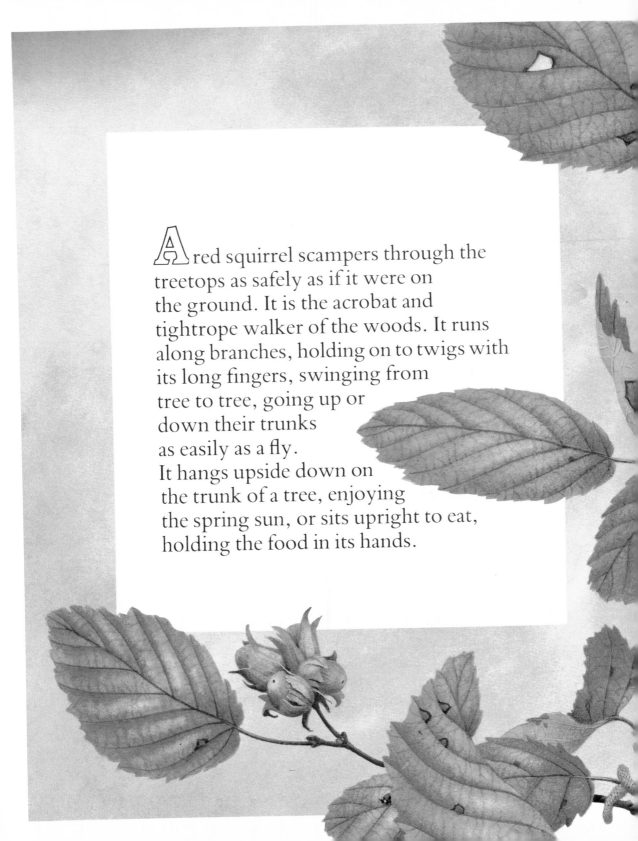

A red squirrel scampers through the treetops as safely as if it were on the ground. It is the acrobat and tightrope walker of the woods. It runs along branches, holding on to twigs with its long fingers, swinging from tree to tree, going up or down their trunks as easily as a fly.
It hangs upside down on the trunk of a tree, enjoying the spring sun, or sits upright to eat, holding the food in its hands.

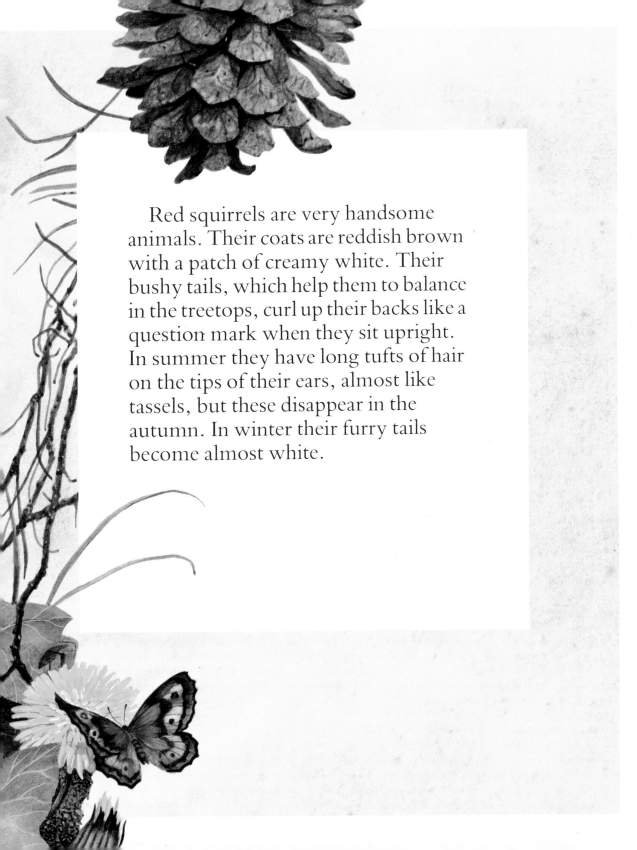

Red squirrels are very handsome animals. Their coats are reddish brown with a patch of creamy white. Their bushy tails, which help them to balance in the treetops, curl up their backs like a question mark when they sit upright. In summer they have long tufts of hair on the tips of their ears, almost like tassels, but these disappear in the autumn. In winter their furry tails become almost white.

Red squirrels live in woods in the United States, Europe, and northern Asia. But gray squirrels, which are tougher and larger, are much more common. Unlike red squirrels, they can live almost anywhere and are seen even in cities.

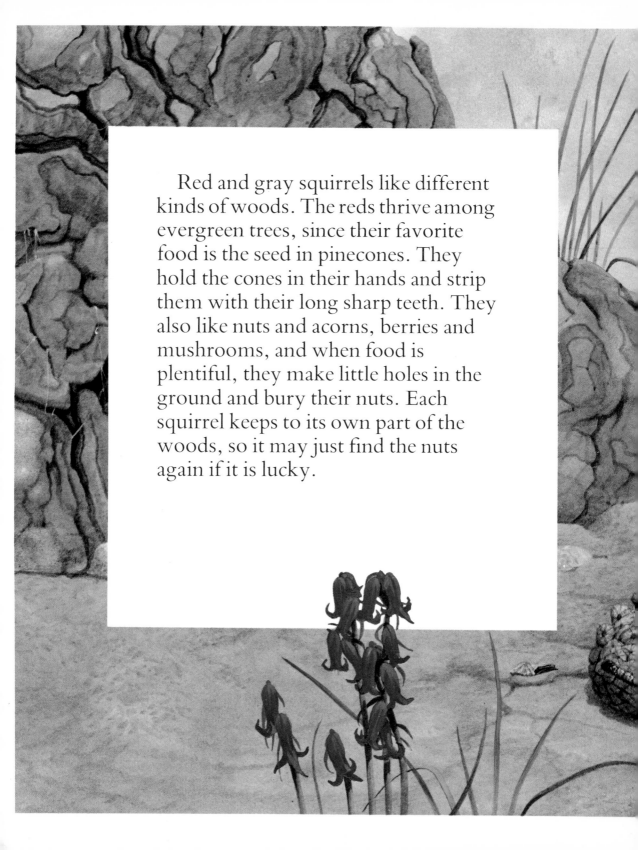

Red and gray squirrels like different kinds of woods. The reds thrive among evergreen trees, since their favorite food is the seed in pinecones. They hold the cones in their hands and strip them with their long sharp teeth. They also like nuts and acorns, berries and mushrooms, and when food is plentiful, they make little holes in the ground and bury their nuts. Each squirrel keeps to its own part of the woods, so it may just find the nuts again if it is lucky.

Gray squirrels, on the other hand, prefer mixed woods of oak, ash, beech, and maple trees, where there are plenty of beechnuts and acorns in autumn and leaf buds and juicy stems at most times of the year. They will also strip bark from a tree to get at the sap beneath. This can damage the tree and make them unpopular with people who live in the country. Gray squirrels also like birds' eggs and will steal them from the nest or even run off with the babies. And they are not above digging up crocus bulbs in gardens.

Both red and gray squirrels are clever builders. They make themselves nests high up in the trees, where they are safe from most enemies. The balloon-shaped nest, made of leaves, twigs, grass, and strips of tree bark, is built among the branches. It has no door, but is so soft and loose that the squirrel can always push its way in or out. Before the birth of her babies a mother squirrel plucks soft fur from her belly to line the nest so that the little ones will be warm and cozy.

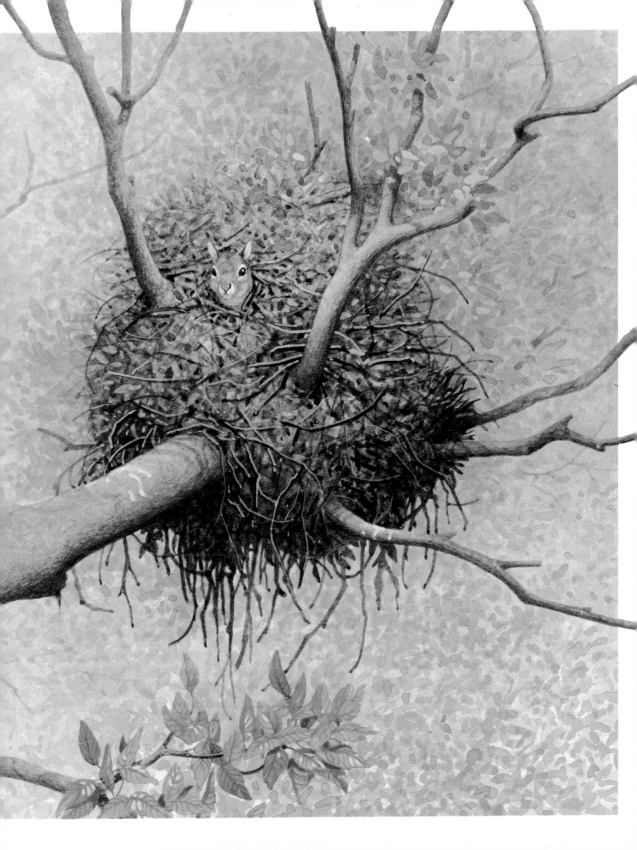

Squirrels choose their mates in early spring. The male scares off any rivals who come near — squeaking, whining, flicking his bushy tail, and rushing around in the branches. If a female appears, he fluffs up his tail and chatters and dances around her. They mate quickly and begin to prepare their nest in the high branches. It will soon be hidden in a screen of green leaves. The baby squirrels, called kittens, will be born in about six weeks.

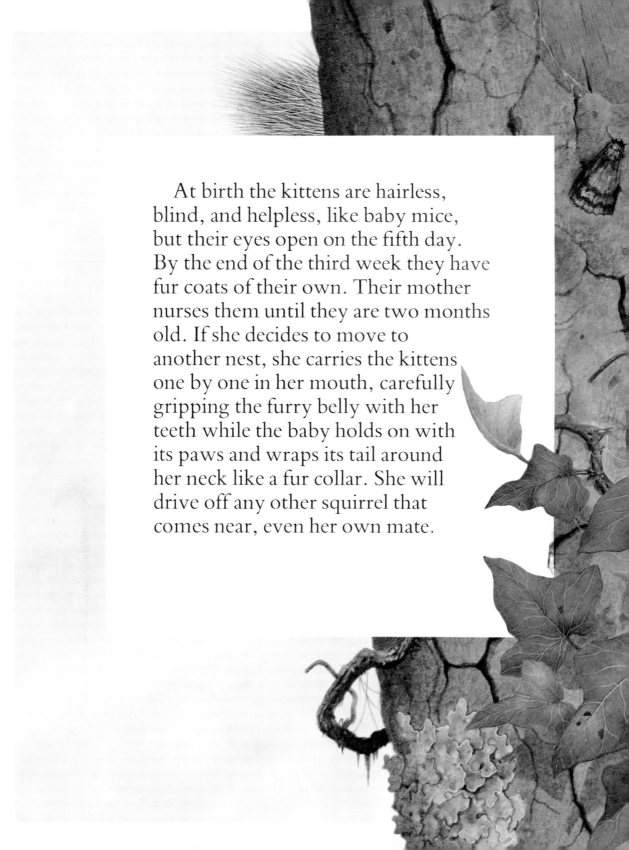

At birth the kittens are hairless, blind, and helpless, like baby mice, but their eyes open on the fifth day. By the end of the third week they have fur coats of their own. Their mother nurses them until they are two months old. If she decides to move to another nest, she carries the kittens one by one in her mouth, carefully gripping the furry belly with her teeth while the baby holds on with its paws and wraps its tail around her neck like a fur collar. She will drive off any other squirrel that comes near, even her own mate.

At ten weeks old the young squirrels need solid food and start exploring the branches on their own. This is their greatest time of danger, when a hawk, a fox, an owl, or even a house cat may suddenly pounce. A young squirrel is a delicious morsel; some people are fond of squirrel meat, which is cooked in a dish called Brunswick stew. But if the kittens are careful, they will probably survive, skipping through the high branches like their parents, gathering nuts, building nests, and soon raising families of their own.

Many people believe that squirrels sleep all winter in their nests, but this is not true. In very cold weather they may stay there for two or three days, keeping warm, but they soon become hungry and come down their trees to hunt for food, even in the snow. At such times they search for nuts and scraps that they have buried. If they live near houses, gray squirrels, hungry and bold, will raid bird feeders. The shy red squirrels are not easily seen in winter in the dark pine woods, yet they are awake. They live off what they can find, or eat pinecones and nuts stored in a hollow tree.

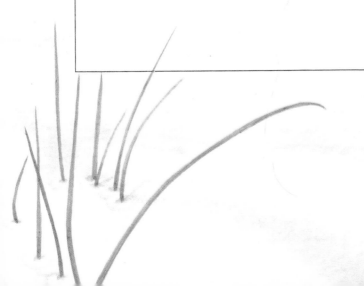

Red and gray squirrels have so many relatives all over the world that it is difficult to count them. There are, in fact, between two and three hundred kinds, all with different names but belonging to the same family. In Africa there are ground squirrels that never go up trees but live in burrows. In the western United States there are woodchucks who dig out vast "towns" of burrows in the open prairie. And all over the country there are chipmunks, small and busy collectors of nuts, with light and dark stripes in their fur.

Many of these relatives, unlike red and gray squirrels, *do* sleep all winter, getting very fat in autumn and waking up thin and hungry in the spring. And there are many flying squirrels, too, both in the north and in the tropics. They perform wonderful gliding leaps from tree to tree by means of a loose fold of skin that spreads out like a rug when they jump. But all squirrels are quick, clever, and agile creatures, making the best of things wherever they happen to be — in woods, mountains, deserts, parks, and suburbs.

About the Author

Margaret Lane is the celebrated author of outstanding books of fiction and biography including *A Night at Sea, A Smell of Burning,* and *The Magic Life of Beatrix Potter.* She has worked as a journalist in London and New York and has written reviews for numerous literary publications.

Ms. Lane was educated at St. Stephen's College in Folkestone, England, and St. Hugh's College, Oxford. She lives with her husband, the 15th Earl of Huntingdon, in Beaulieu, England.

About the Artist

Kenneth Lilly is a well-known British artist whose paintings of animals have been shown in European and American galleries. He was born in Bromley, England, and studied animal anatomy at Sidcup College.

Mr. Lilly lives in Devon, England, with his wife and three children.